WORDS

FROM

BIRDS

Inspiration from our Feathered Friends

Author,
Tawnya Shaffer

WORDS FROM BIRDS

Unless otherwise noted, all scripture quotations are from The Thompson Chain-Reference Bible New International Version, copyright ©1983 by The B.B. Kirkbride Bible Co. Inc. and The Zondervan Corporation.

Copyright©2017 Tawnya Shaffer
All rights reserved.

Dedication Page

This collection of devotions comes from years of researching, observing and admiring the nature of birds, their habits and their relativity to us. It is also from years of urging by my dear family to put these into print form for others to enjoy. Lastly and most importantly it is in obedience to my dear Lord for asking me to take my writing to the next level.

So, this work is first dedicated to the God who inspires and gives me my words and in hopes that the ears who receive it will be challenged and changed.

Secondly, to my dear husband of 30 years, Dennis. I love you with my whole being and celebrate the ups and downs we have had for they color my writing with the faithfulness of our God. Love you babe, thanks for being my biggest cheerleader!

Thirdly, to my amazing children; Zachary, Andrea, Justin and Jordyn, it is and always will be a privilege to be your mom. Your eagle qualities make me so very proud every day and I am so incredibly blessed to watch you blossom into adults and navigate your personal journeys. I love you all so much!

Fourth, to my precious grandbabies; Lane Paul and Leena Bug. You bring so much joy and laughter to me and all that meet you. Nana loves you!

Last, to all my family and friends who have encouraged me through the years to put my spoken word into book form. Thanks for your undying support and encouragement. May this be the first of many books to come and may each bring glory to the only deserving one, our mighty God!

Love, Tawnya

WORDS FROM BIRDS

Table of Contents

Dedication page	3
Blue Bully (Blue Jay)	6
Two is Better than One (Eagle)	8
Drowning in the Storm (Turkey)	12
Nest Built on High (Eagle)	14
My Warbler Friend (Warbler)	16
Eagle Eyes (Eagle)	18
Sandwich Snatcher (Seagull)	22
Let's Soar (Eagle)	24
Vulgar Vulture (Vulture)	28
Fly Above the Storm (Eagle)	32
Heads Up (Ostrich)	34
Caring for the Wounded (Eagle)	36
Pretty in Pink (Flamingo)	38
Check Your Oil (Eagle)	42
Off Balance Bird (Pelican)	44
Mama Knows Best (Eagle)	48
Amen, Hallelujah, Praise the Lord (Parrot)	52
Worn (Eagle)	56
Shut Your Beak (Vulture)	58
Captivity or Freedom? (Eagle)	60
Let the Water Roll Off (Duck)	64
Fiercely Committed (Eagle)	68
Wave Runner Attack (Swan)	72
Flight School (Eagle)	76
A Call to Remember (Mourning Dove)	80
Built in GPS (Eagle)	84
Victim of a Dive Attack (Killdeer)	88
Fresh Meat Please (Eagle)	92
The Un Bird (Penguin)	96
Flying Solo (Eagle)	100

"Blue Bully"

As a young girl, I enjoyed watching the bird feeder out our bay kitchen window and I particularly enjoyed the variety of feathered friends. That variety was quickly disrupted by one culprit. A beautiful, stately bird to watch, the blue jay was one of my favorites. He was so pretty with his blue feathers trimmed in black and set off by his white belly. As beautiful as he was, the blue jay was equally mean and viewed the bird feeder as his own. I watched him dive, peck and run countless birds away from the bird feeder even if they were there first. This possessive quality caused him to chase away all the other chick-a-dees, swallows and hummingbirds. The blue jay wanted the feeder and seed to himself and scared the others away.

The church today is full of blue jay Christians---eager to drive out anyone different to maintain his "feeder" or church as his own. The church, the building and no certain pew belongs to any one person.... they all belong to God. The church is comprised of imperfect people just like you and me. None of us truly deserves God's grace, it doesn't matter what color our tail feathers are or what our past holds. It is God's goodness and love that saves us, not anything we have earned. In fact, the more birds of a different feather that come in the doors the better. Isn't it our goal to bring the lost to Christ? So why are we chasing them away with our judgments? Don't be a bully blue jay Christian…. open your arms and heart and welcome others to the feeder.

Seed from the Feeder: Matthew 22:39 "Love your neighbor as yourself."

Flap or Fly? Step out of your comfort zone. The next time you see someone that is different or may feel out of place at church…make a move and welcome him! Help that person feel a part of the feeder!

FEATHERED FACT: The bird's name derives from its noisy, garrulous nature, and it is also called a "jaybird".

Photo Credit- Matt Day

"Two is Better than One"

Eagle parents are a team when it comes to raising their young from the day the eggs are laid, until the young leave the nest, and even beyond. The female eagle produces one to four eggs one at a time, with 2 to 3 days between eggs. Because the female takes a while to lay her eggs, she is also the one to initially incubate them. But Daddy is not kicking back in a recliner. The male brings food to the nest for the female and even brings fresh evergreen or branches for the soon to be or newly hatched eaglets. After the initial period, both parents share the incubation duties for the 34-36 days until the hatching begins. The young hatch in the order that they were laid and similar to the laying period, it can be 2-3 days between each eaglet emerges from their egg.

Feeding of the young is a team effort. I had the privilege this spring of watching a live eagle-cam from Alcoa Nature Preserve in Iowa and repeatedly saw both parents bringing, tearing and offering food to the eager little ones. My favorite moments of observing were when both parents were present at the same time and the family was together for a meal. If one parent goes hunting, the other stays at the nest but the mom and dad both do hunting; they are in it together.

The young eagles start to take flight at about 10-12 weeks but the initial flights can be rough. It is usually 10- 15 weeks after they actually are flying when they consider leaving their parents. During this "adolescence" phase the parents do not abandon the young. They follow them around and bring them food while they are in flight training. Even when the young eagles are flying well, the parents continue to model how to hunt and how to survive in the winter. Some young eagles are in the same vicinity for up to five years.

With divorce being at a rate of 1 out of 2 marriages, even in Christian homes, we need to learn from the eagle. God designed parenting to require a man and a woman to become a father and a mother. Children need both parents to grow and develop to the best of their abilities. If you want to challenge this, visit a prison and ask the inmates how many of them came from broken homes, the statistics are staggering, trust me. With parenting two is truly better than one.

Seed from the Feeder: Deuteronomy 11:18 "Teach them to your children, talking about them when you sit at home and when you walk along the road, when you lie down and when you get up."

Flap or Fly? Are you a parent? How are you doing with your God given responsibilities? The world is changing but one area that should not change is parenting. Take time to really talk with your kids, teach them about God, and show them that they are loved!

FEATHERED FACT: During a lot of the final weeks in the nest, the young birds play tug of war with each other, using sticks and parts of leftover meals.

Photo Credit- Tawnya Shaffer

∞ **Reflection Page** ∞

Journal your thoughts: _____

_____

_____

_____

_____

_____

God, help me to: _____

_____

_____

_____

Thank you Lord for: _____

_____

_____

_____

My prayer requests/ answers: _____

_____

_____

_____

"Drowning in the Storm"

Turkeys are very popular and well-loved birds especially at Thanksgiving. Few people realize how ignorant this succulent fowl can be when facing a storm. Turkey farmers know this fact and realize it is imperative to put their flock inside before the rain begins. Why? Other birds remain outside in the rain, snow and cold and seem fine. So why does the turkey have to be put up?

During a storm, that colorful Tom turkey will unbelievably stand statue-like, mouth up and literally drown himself in the rain. This is more prominent in young turkeys and is due to the angle that the bird holds its head. If a turkey gets the head too far back, it cannot swallow and will inadvertently drown. The turkey literally becomes paralyzed at the sight of rain and will not survive if the farmer doesn't intervene.

You may chuckle at this idiosyncrasy but think about how many humans are just like this bird. We can be easily paralyzed by the storms in our lives. When the rain starts, we stand still, become paralyzed by circumstances and before we know it we are drowning in sorrow, anger or bitterness. We cannot control the storm, but we can control how we react to the storm!

Divorce, illness, a rebelling child, an unexpected tragedy are all examples of how we can be blindsided by life. God is our farmer and desires to take you out of the weather or comfort you through it. He is our refuge if we allow him to be. It is not necessary to try and survive on our own; we have a God who loves and cares about us in all situations. Are the storms of life drowning you today? Look to your keeper who will care for you through the storm. Don't drown, look to the crown.

Seed from the Feeder: Psalm 46:1 "God is our refuge and strength, an ever-present help in trouble."

Flap or Fly? What storm have you tried to weather alone? Give any bitterness, anger or resentment to Jesus today. He is here to save you from the storm.

FEATHERED FACT: The average lifespan for a domesticated turkey is ten years.

Photo Credit- Justyce Chapman

WORDS FROM BIRDS

"Nest Built on High"

The eagle's home is as impressive as its wingspan. This nest is no small feat to create. The eagle builds the largest nest of any North American bird. To start the eagle first selects a strong, firm foundation for its formidable home. A typical building site is a tall firm tree or a rocky crag or cliff side. It is usually built near a body of water with great visibility for hunting. Wherever it is, it must be strong…. very strong! The typical eagle's nest is eight to ten feet wide and twenty feet deep and can weigh up to two tons!! A firm foundation is imperative for that impressive of a home.

This place of residence needs strength and durability to last. Most eagle nests are used and inhabited by the same set of parents for about thirty years. Through the life of the nest, it is constantly added to and reinforced which gives it the large size. Eagles average one-three eggs per year…. that is a lot of eaglets raised within its walls. The strength makes a dependable home and the height where the eagles build it makes it safe from predators and danger while Pa and Ma Eagle are out hunting for their offspring.

How is your foundation? Is it built on high with Jesus Christ? Is it firm and safe from predators? Does it provide a safe haven for your children and generations to come? You don't have to have been saved for over 50 years to achieve this foundation. Once a decision for Christ is made, your trust is on the rock! With Christ, you gain power and protection from the predators of this world. And like the eagle's nest…. this home is made to last, not just for thirty years, but for an eternity! Put your trust in Christ today and build a foundation worthy of an eagle.

Seed from the Feeder: Job 39:27-28 "Is it at your command that the eagle mounts up and makes his nest on high? On the rock, he dwells and makes his home, on the rocky crag and stronghold."

Flap or Fly? How is your foundation……shaky or firm? Make a choice today to give Christ total control of your life, all decisions and relationships should be His to control.

FEATHERED FACT: One nest in Florida was found to be 6.1 meters (20 ft.) deep, 2.9 meters (9.5 ft.) across, and weighing 3 short tons.

Photo Credit- Tawnya Shaffer

"My Warbler Friend"

Relaxing in the sun in Florida, I was stunned to see a small gray and yellow warbler land less than a foot from my face. He perched proudly on a small bush and looked me in the eye. Tilting his head, he chirped quietly with his bright yellow beak. Obviously, not feeling great alarm, my visitor remained for a few minutes fluffing his feathers and self-preening. Before I knew it, I was surrounded by six other feathered friends who were searching the mulch for an afternoon snack. Some were skittish, others, like my friend appeared content with my company.

Similar behavior can be found in the church or Christian setting. Many "birds" are comfortable, content to sit and preen themselves. Others are extremely skittish and uncomfortable, prepared to take flight any minute. While another group is feverishly busy working.

Where do you fall? The preeners are too occupied with bettering themselves with scripture memorization and study to reach out to the lost. Please don't get me wrong, scripture memory is a great thing unless you choose not to heed its instruction. The skittish flock has typically had a bad experience with church or doesn't feel worthy to be inside the walls. The workers are doing what they can to expand the kingdom of God but quite frankly are getting tired doing it all themselves.

Are you comfortable with your Father looking down at you? Are you busy self-preening or are you in the group working for others? Maybe you are in the flock that has never found a comfortable, accepting church home and wants to take flight at even the mention of God. Please know that your Father is lovingly looking down on you, wanting you to embrace His love and to work for His kingdom. Don't take flight, find hope in Christ!

Seed from the Feeder: Colossians 3:23 "Whatever you do, work at it with all your heart, as working for the Lord not for men."

Flap or Fly? Find a balance today…..read and study God's Word AND do what it says…reach the lost, especially those who are skittish and have walked away from the church.

FEATHERED FACT: The two families of American "warblers" are part of another superfamily, which unites them with sparrows, buntings, finches.

Photo Credit- pixabay.com

WORDS FROM BIRDS

"Eagle Eyes"

If a person has an astounding ability to see they are often labeled an "eagle eye". That phrase is a huge compliment to the eagle, its visual abilities and is entirely accurate. The eagle's eye has a unique tubular shape which increases its acuity. How much do you ask? Well an eagle can see two miles from any direction. They can also focus from two feet to two miles extremely rapidly, this is called accommodation and the eagle is an expert at it. The ability to quickly change focus is one of the reasons that the eagle is such a great hunter and can see fish under water. The eagle can spot fish underwater from several hundred feet in the air. The eagle also has a second eyelid that comes down to protect from injury and acts similar to our sunglasses so that the eagle can fly directly towards the sun.

Vision is one of the five senses but it is also "the ability to anticipate possible future events or developments" (Encarta). Seeing with our eyes is extremely important but having vision for the future is vital to God's plan. God has a plan for each of our lives and we are instrumental to a greater design. But if we are not in tune to the

Father, we may miss the vision He has for us. Helen Keller once said "To have eyes and no vision is worse than being blind." This was coming from a woman who had been blind her entire life.

We need to strive to be like the eagle. The eagle flies toward the sun. When is the last time you tuned in to the Son? Are you open to promptings in your life that God has placed there? These may be as simple as going up to a complete stranger and encouraging them or it may be a deeper calling like ministry. The higher the eagle goes, the greater their vision. How high are you going with your walk with Christ? Are you satisfied to just attend church once in a while, or are you ready to be used as God intended? The eagle is a bird with unmatched vision and all of us that are children of God can have a different type but equally great vision. Are you willing to be an eagle eye?

Seed from the Feeder: Job 39:29 "From there he seeks out his food; his eyes detect it from afar."

Flap or Fly? What vision do you have? What is God asking you to do? We are the hands and feet of Christ and he will use us to change many lives but we have to have vision. The key is to go higher in your walk and then you can see more clearly. It is time to soar!

WORDS FROM BIRDS

FEATHERED FACT: Eagles, like all birds, have color vision. An eagle's eye is almost as large as a human's, but its sharpness is at least four times that of a person with perfect vision. The eagle can probably identify a rabbit moving almost a mile away. That means that an eagle flying at an altitude of 1000 feet over open country could spot prey over an area of almost 3 square miles from a fixed position.

Photo credit- Tawnya Shaffer

∞ **Reflection Page** ∞

Journal your thoughts: _____

_____
_____
_____
_____
_____
_____

God, help me to: _____

_____
_____
_____
_____

Thank you Lord for: _____

_____
_____
_____
_____

My prayer requests/ answers: _____

_____
_____
_____

WORDS FROM BIRDS

"Sandwich Snatcher"

"Gorgeous" best describes the day my husband and I were having at Clearwater Beach as we shared a picnic lunch on a blanket. It was perfect except one thing. That thing was a pearl white, picturesque sea gull. Sure, he was pretty to look at until he swooped down from behind me and literally snatched my sandwich out of my hand. I had only had one bite from that half and his antics left me hungry and irritated! Carefully guarding what remained on my plate, I ate with watchful eyes although my belly was not satisfied.

Sea gulls are beautiful birds that are found near or on bodies of water. They feed on fish, insects and apparently, human's sandwiches. Many of these big soaring water fowl are accustomed to human contact and will come very near if it means being fed. Travelers unfamiliar with the gulls' antics will eagerly feed these birds with hopes of obtaining a picture or memory. Little do those tourists realize if you feed one gull, you will soon be entertaining an entire flock. When my sandwich flew away in the beak of the thief, it was instantly fought over by more than 30 others. My gull friend needed meat.

As Christians, we are to be eating spiritual meat daily. Like my seagull friend there are countless distractions that snatch away our time with God. Those items may appear harmless like a job, family, children's events, housework and even church. It doesn't matter how well-meaning these tasks are, if they are getting in the way of God time they are thieves. Regardless of what your snatcher is, without that daily spiritual meal you will be left irritated, unsatisfied and hungry for God's teachings. I should have better guarded my sandwich and we should all be more careful to keep anything from stealing our precious time with the Father.

What is on your daily plate? Does it include a daily dose of spiritual meat? Or is something snatching it away?

Seed from the Feeder: Matthew 6:33 "But seek *FIRST* His kingdom and his righteousness, and all these things will be given to you as well."

Flap or Fly? Take a minute to reflect on the amount of time you spend in God's Word every day. Now honestly consider what you can change to increase those God moments. Eliminate one or two of your sandwich snatchers….is it TV, computer time or overtime? Commit to make the change now!

FEATHERED FACT: Certain species of gulls have been noted to use a piece of bread to bait small fish. This tactic is called tool use behavior.

Photo credit- Tawnya Shaffer

WORDS FROM BIRDS

"Let's Soar!"

One summer I had the privilege of seeing nine bald eagles at various times, some young and some old, in their natural habitats, flying, perching and soaring majestically. If you have never had the privilege, it is a sight to behold. I have spotted this majestic creature in lower and upper Michigan and in my present state of Indiana. When you see the grace and power of a bald eagle in full flight, you will not quickly forget it. The eagle is mentioned in scripture over 26 times, more than any other bird. Why do you suppose? Because the eagle's characteristics compared to other birds are unmatched. One of those is its ability to soar.

The eagle has an impressive wing span of 7 to 9 feet and has four more total flight feathers than any other raptors, which assist in soaring. Eagles can take off from a standing position with only 1-2 flaps of its wings and off the water's surface with additional 1-2 flaps. The average speed of an eagle in flight is 30 to 35 mph but those speeds can easily increase to 65 mph. When an eagle is in a dive it will reach speeds of more than 100mph! These majestic birds can fly low over water or can reach altitudes of 10,000 feet. Using the currents of the wind and gliding with them, the eagle can stay aloft for hours.

Consider for a moment what would happen if the eagle was a flapper. Just what would it look like to see a bird with that great of a wing span flapping? It would not be natural and the eagle would quickly tire. He knows that to fly effectively he needs to use the wind and its currents to help it soar.

Many of us are "flappers", me included. We try to do everything in our own power. We flap like crazy trying to fix this and make that happen when we are meant to soar. Like the eagle uses the strength of the wind to soar, Christians need to use the power of God to lift and carry us. Are you wasting your energy flapping through life? Spread your wings, allow God to lift you and SOAR!

Seed from the Feeder: Exodus 19:4 "You yourselves have seen what I did to Egypt, and how I carried you on eagles' wings and brought you to myself"

Flap or Fly? What are you struggling with today? Are your wings tired of flapping? Open the wings that God gave you, bow at His feet and allow Him to take the load and start to soar today.

FEATHERED FACT: The tail of the eagle is an important device for maneuvering, slowing down and increasing surface area while in flight. This amazing tail works much like the rudders on an airplane.

Photo Credit- Zachary Shaffer

∞ **Reflection Page** ∞

Journal your thoughts: _____

_____
_____
_____
_____
_____

God, help me to: _____

_____
_____
_____

Thank you Lord for: _____

_____
_____
_____

My prayer requests/ answers: _____

_____
_____
_____

"Vulgar Vulture"

Have you ever really had the opportunity to examine a vulture? As much as I love birds, I can't bring myself to find the vulture attractive. His habits are as vulgar as his appearance. A vulture eats off dead and rotting carcasses. He doesn't know how long his meal has been lying on the side off the road and how many other animals have eaten off it. The vulture does not care. Much of what is consumed by this ugly bird is full of toxins and decaying substances.

The vulture is weak because it does not have to pursue or kill its prey. A vulture's talons are used to tear at the meat that is lying in wait for consumption. The talons are not used to kill the way the eagle or hawk's talons are utilized. A vulture will circle an anticipated meal to be sure it is dead to avoid having to finish the kill. If a prey's hide is too thick, the vulture will wait and circle until a stronger attacker breaks the hide and carcass open.

Have you ever heard the expression "you are what you eat?" This is true for the vulture and for the Christian. What are you putting into your body? I am not necessarily talking food. What about the music, books, and media that you are allowing to penetrate your ears and eyes? Are you feeding off the filth of life? We need to meditate on what is holy and honorable so we can emanate Christ and His love to others.

Similar to the vulture, the longer we maintain these unhealthy habits, the weaker we become spiritually. How long have you been preying on toxins and decaying substances? Are your talons weak because you haven't been sharpening them with scripture and regular Christ based teaching? It is often the secret habits we maintain that emulate the vulture but remember, secret or not, these habits will show somewhere in our life. If you are feeding on the filth of life…. you will emulate that externally. Do you want to exhibit toxins or Christ in your life? It is your choice!

Seed from the Feeder: 1 Corinthians 6:19 & 20 "Do you not know that your body is a temple of the Holy Spirit, who is in you, whom you have received from God? You are bought at a price. Therefore, honor God with your body."

Flap or Fly? Music and pictures on the computer can seem harmless but the immoral messages and mind pictures that they deliver can be very difficult to erase. Be diligent in making wise choices for yourself and your family.

WORDS FROM BIRDS

FEATHERED FACT: Vulture stomach acid is exceptionally corrosive, allowing it to safely digest putrid carcasses infected with Botulin toxin, hog cholera, and anthrax bacteria that would be lethal to other scavengers.

Photo credit- Tawnya Shaffer

∞ **Reflection Page** ∞

Journal your thoughts: _____

_____

_____

_____

_____

_____

God, help me to: _____

_____

_____

_____

Thank you Lord for: _____

_____

_____

_____

My prayer requests/ answers: _____

_____

_____

_____

"Fly Above the Storm"

An eagle, like many animals can sense an approaching storm but it does not run from it. The eagle understands the storm, its power, and its positive attributes. This giant bird is aware that the currents of the storm can work to its advantage. Understanding this, the eagle flies above the storm allowing the powerful undercurrents to carry him.

An eagle's ability to soar is not entirely his own but largely due to the air currents. It uses rising air called thermals to lift itself and can stay aloft for much longer with less effort. An eagle's average air speed is 36-44 mph with top diving speeds reaching 100 mph or more. As a storm approaches, the eagle feels the change in the air currents and actually anticipates the arrival of the system and a great opportunity to soar higher and longer.

The human response to the storms of life is typically very different from the eagle. We tend to mimic the chicken or the turkey by running or becoming paralyzed by trials of life. We can learn much from the eagle including that the storm can be a positive force in our life. By modeling the eagle's response to changes in life we gain wisdom, character, perseverance and hope and can endure and fly above the storms we face.

Where are you today? Are you flapping under the torrents of the trials in your life or are you soaring above with Christ carrying you?

Seed from the Feeder: James 1:2-3 "Consider it pure joy my brothers whenever you face trials of many kinds because you know that the testing of your faith develops perseverance."

Flap or Fly? What storms have you endured in the last five years? Are you still reeling from the pain and effects of it? Did you choose to grow from it? Talk to God about your recent responses to trials. Commit to face your next adversity like the eagle.

FEATHERED FACT: The plumage of the young eagle does not attain its white color until maturity at five years of age which protects it from predators until strong enough to defend itself.

Photo credit- Pam Oberski

"Heads Up"

The ostrich is the world's largest bird and never leaves the ground. Most people relate the ostrich to its defensive behaviors of sticking its head in the ground. Contrary to popular belief, ostriches do not entirely bury their heads in the sand. The old saying probably originates from what this large bird does when threatened. At the approach of trouble, ostriches will lie low and press their long necks to the ground in an attempt to become less visible. Their plumage blends well with sandy soil and, from a distance, gives the appearance that they have buried their heads in the sand. Now keep in mind the ostrich can run as fast as 43 MPH and has legs strong enough to kick and kill a human or a lion. True the bird can't fly but it could defend itself in other ways but it chooses to stop, lower its head and try to disappear.

My husband and I worked with teenagers for many years and one of the hardest challenges for them was to stand up for Jesus in the presence of their peers. Being a confessing and practicing Christian can jeopardize popularity and acceptance for adults but especially for teenagers. Instead of verbally telling others about

Christ, these young adults choose to lower their heads and just blend in with their surroundings. Like the ostrich, they have other options. They are promised the power and help of the Holy Spirit but take a way out that seems easiest.

How about you? Are you blending in with co-workers, family members & friends or are you choosing to stand up for what you believe? You many think that lowering your head is the best approach but consider how many opportunities you may be passing up to share Jesus with someone who may not have another occasion to hear the good news. Life is not about being easy or comfortable. It is about fulfilling the plan of Christ to save as many lost souls as possible! So get your head out of the sand and make a difference!

Seed from the Feeder: Matthew 10:32-33 "Whoever acknowledges me before men, I will also acknowledge him before my Father in heaven. But whoever disowns me before men, I will disown him before my Father in heaven."

Flap or Fly? Can you think of the last time you had to make a choice to amplify or deny Christ? It can be tough to be the different one in the crowd, but God's Word is clear… we need to stand up for Him and not deny Him.

FEATHERED FACT: The ostrich has the largest eye of any land animal. It measures approximately 2 inches across.

Photo Credit- Tawnya Shaffer

WORDS FROM BIRDS

"Caring for the Wounded"

Midlife the eagle experiences a physical crisis and a chemical change takes place in his body. Due to this "midlife crisis" the eagle becomes weak and isolates itself away from other eagles on the floor of a valley. The poor, once majestic bird lays head down, eyes dry, lifeless as its feathers begin to fall out one at a time. Losing hope, the eagle faces sure death......UNTIL...

Suddenly the ill bird hears something from above. It looks up to see a circle formation of fellow eagles calling to him. *Are they mocking me? Will they attack me when I am down?* These are thoughts that may pass through the eagle's mind during this uncertain time.

About to give up, the eagle lowers its head in despair when morsels of food begin to drop around him. As the days pass, the circle of friends continues to feed, protect and support their wounded comrade. Before long strength is renewed, feathers re-grow and the eagle is once again able to soar!

As a church, we should mimic this behavior. There are countless situations that our fellow believers experience that leave them lifeless and wounded. What is our response when our comrades fall? Do we gossip and further wound them or do we nourish, support and uphold them? The church of all locations should be a place of refuge and healing but repeatedly we kick those who are down by judging their sin or spreading their misfortune around the community. How are you caring for the wounded eagles around you?

Seed from the Feeder: John 21:16 "Again Jesus said, "Simon, son of John do you truly love me?" He answered, "Yes, Lord, you know that I love you." Jesus said, "Take care of my sheep."

Flap or Fly? Think about the fellow "eagles" that are hurting right now. Make a plan to reach out and care for them in at least one specific way this week, then make a habit to care for hurting people regularly.

FEATHERED FACT: An eagle's size varies by type, sex, and geographic location but on average the wingspan is between 5.9- 7.5 feet and weighs between 5.5- 17 lbs.

Photo Credit- Tawnya Shaffer

WORDS FROM BIRDS

"Pretty in Pink"

While visiting a Florida theme park it was hard to miss the colorful, impressive collection of bright pink flamingos standing statue-like. They screamed "look at me", "aren't I pretty", and "I am superior" to anyone who glanced their way. It almost appeared that their beauty permitted them to be motionless, with one leg tucked up under their bellies; they did not intend to take flight anytime soon. The flamingo is a very social bird and stays with its flock, all flaunting themselves in the same prideful manner, their nose in the air… but nothing else as they stand instead of flying.

Can you translate into human terms? After 23 years of ministry in various churches, I can. One large congregation with a lot of great people comes to mind. Like any group of people, Christian or not, there were those who dressed "just so", drove the latest model of never dirty sedans, and were squeaky clean from the outside. These flamingo Christians were full of pride, and typically gathered with others just like them…. their flock. Unfortunately, this flock was also good at looking down at others who didn't measure up. They were so worried about appearances that their disapproving glances toward not-so-fortunate visitors kept others from being saved. Like the flamingo does not fly as birds are intended to, these pride-filled Christians did not fulfill their responsibility to bring others Jesus.

As Christians, we are not superior, we are forgiven! It is not about how we dress or what type of house we live in or the cars we drive. All that God is concerned about with is the condition of your heart. Are you too impressed with self to be concerned with others? Or do you see a need, and regardless of the cost, you fill it, putting others before yourself? Let Jesus be our standard of self-centered attitudes. Look at his life and ask yourself did He ever stand still flaunting himself, did He travel in flocks or was He fine with flying alone when necessary? Pride does not seem as horrific as murder, adultery, or a host of other sins but the trail of damage it can leave is as destructive. Choose today to be Christ-like, not pink.

Seed from the Feeder: Matthew 23:6-8 & 12 "They love the place of honor at banquets and the most important seats in the synagogues; they love to be greeted in the marketplace and to have men call them Rabbi. But you are not to be called Rabbi for you have only one Master and you are all brothers." "For whoever exalts himself will be humbled, and whoever humbles himself will be exalted."

WORDS FROM BIRDS

Flap or Fly? Ask yourself what do you do for yourself, and then ask yourself what you do for others on a daily basis. The Pharisees wanted to be honored and exalted instead of minister to others. Are you acting more like a Pharisee or more like Jesus?

FEATHERED FACT: Flamingos use their long legs and webbed feet to stir up the bottom. They then bury their bills, or even their entire heads, and suck up both mud and water to access the tasty morsels within. A flamingo's beak has a filter like structure to remove food from the water before the liquid is expelled.

Photo Credit- Pixabay

∞ Reflection Page ∞

Journal your thoughts: _____

_____

_____

_____

_____

_____

God, help me to: _____

_____

_____

_____

Thank you Lord for: _____

_____

_____

_____

My prayer requests/ answers: _____

_____

_____

_____

"Check your Oil"

The eagle is very ritualistic with his daily hygiene and part of that routine includes the use of special oil. Every day the giant bird spends about an hour grooming each feather on its wings. This is no small task knowing that there are over 1,250 feathers on each wing. The eagle breathes and blows out the dirt and residue. Then he reaches behind his tail where there is a special gland that excretes oil. That oil is crucial, and is placed by the eagle on each feather to complete the preening process.

The routine is time well spent and protects the eagle through the coming day. By breathing through the feathers, he cleans them and avoids them matting together which could affect flight. The oil waterproofs the feathers so that in any kind of weather, the eagle can soar unaffected by moisture. If the eagle chose to skip this necessary process, flight, hunting and even its survival could be affected.

What most Christians fail to realize is that much of our life is dependent on a preening process that we frequently abandon for other priorities. Time with God in prayer, reading the Word, and just listening for His direction is essential to our daily existence. We need to breathe the dirt out of our life and routinely apply a spiritual oil of protection. Why is it so easy to allow this preening process to remain undone for days, weeks, and even months? Yet we are surprised when we falter, face and fail challenges, but have taken no time to oil up. Take some valuable time to preen…. you will fly so much better!

Seed from the Feeder: 2 Timothy 3:16 & 17 "All Scripture is God-breathed and is useful for teaching, rebuking, correcting and training in righteousness, so that the man of God may be thoroughly equipped for every good work."

Flap or Fly? How is your personal devotion time? Could it use a bit of preening? When is the last time you applied some "spiritual oil" or good scripture knowledge to your tail feathers? Make some personal goals to start preening some every day.

FEATHERED FACT: A typical adult bald eagle has more than 7,000 total feathers.

Photo Credit- Rachel Pearch

"Off Balance Bird"

    Being at the beach is without question my favorite destination for many reasons. One of those reasons is being entertained by the brown pelicans that fly back and forth parallel to the beach in search of their next meal. These large billed birds will be in flight and then "Bam" they take a dive into the water, beaks open to grab the fish in their sight. From my perspective, I can never tell if the diving hunter has attained their goal or not but it sure is fun to watch them try.

    As entertaining as the pelican is to watch, they do have a downfall. They scoop up food and don't know when to stop. They get so many fish that they can't eat it all. This little habit can go to the extreme of having so many fish in their beak that they become off balance and can't fly properly. What a shame! A bird that flies so beautifully, and has the ability to cut and dive can impair itself to the point of not being able to get off the ground. That just shouldn't be.

    Christians mimic this same behavior when we become "Fat" Christians. What does that mean? Feeding ourselves by going to church, small groups, Bible studies and personal devotions is all honorable behavior. Bible memorization and knowing scripture helps us to prepare for our daily walk. Let me ask you what happens when we eat too much physically and don't exercise? We gain weight, right? Sure. The same is true in our Christian walk; if we just feed ourselves spiritually and don't exercise we become spiritually fat. If we don't take what we learn and put action to all that knowledge it is all a waste.

It is amazing to me when people have the mindset that the church is there to serve them. That type of thinking is so backwards. We exist to serve. We exist to share the love and the message of Christ. Hiding God's Word in your heart does absolutely no good if lives are not changed. Do you have a full beak? Are you off balance and unable to fly because you are spiritually fat? Time to get some spiritual exercise!

Seed from the Feeder: Mark 16:15 "Go into all the world and preach the good news to all creation."

Flap or Fly? When is the last time that you put scripture into action? Have you told someone about Jesus? Have you cared for someone in need? Have you forgiven someone recently? Don't get fat… read scripture and then be doers!

WORDS FROM BIRDS

FEATHERED FACT: The American white pelican can hold some 3 gallons (11 1/2 liters) of water in its bill. Young pelicans feed by sticking their bills into their parents' throats to retrieve food.

Photo Credit- Zachary Shaffer

∞ **Reflection Page** ∞

Journal your thoughts: _____

_____

_____

_____

_____

_____

God, help me to: _____

_____

_____

_____

Thank you Lord for: _____

_____

_____

_____

My prayer requests/ answers: _____

_____

_____

_____

WORDS FROM BIRDS

"Mama Knows Best"

Parent eagles share child-rearing responsibilities equally and work together on preparing the young for leaving the nest. As the eaglets progressively get older, the parent eagles return to the nest fewer and fewer times, to drop off food but also to start to encourage independence. At about 3 months of age (1-2 months before the eaglets will leave the nest) the mother eagle makes a slight adjustment to the nest that is important to prepare her little ones for their journey from the nest.

There is a soft, down layer mixed with evergreen needles that cushion the little ones during their first weeks of life. At three months of age Mama knows junior may be getting too comfortable so she makes a change. She starts to sweep the soft cover out of the nest. You may think this is cruel but like any mother, she has a method to her madness. By removing this coating, it forces the little ones to stand more…. strengthening their legs and conditioning their talons. This forced fitness is essential to prepare them for their upcoming first flights.

The parent eagles know what the first months of life hold for their offspring and will do what needs to be done to prepare them for life outside the nest. God is our Father and He also knows what is best for us. He, like the eagle, knows what the future hold for his children and prepares them in ways that He understands. Unfortunately, we may not always understand His ways and may question circumstances we encounter. I am sure the eaglets complain a bit when their soft nest is altered but little do they know it is for their own good. We need to trust that our Father loves us and knows what is best for us too. When life doesn't seem comfortable, remember it may be like Mama sweeping the nest and Mama always knows best!

Seed from the Feeder: Proverbs 3:5 & 6 "Trust in the Lord with all your heart and lean not on your own understanding; in all your ways acknowledge him and he will make your paths straight."

Flap or Fly? Trust God with all aspects in your life, even if something you are going through seems very uncomfortable. Trust God to forgive your yesterdays, guide your todays and prepare your tomorrows!

FEATHERED FACT: If an eagle miscalculates and misses its target while fishing, there is no need to worry, its hollow feathers function like a life jacket and prevent the bird from sinking

WORDS FROM BIRDS

Photo Credit- Rachel Pearch

∞ **Reflection Page** ∞

Journal your thoughts: _____

_____

_____

_____

_____

_____

God, help me to: _____

_____

_____

_____

_____

Thank you Lord for: _____

_____

_____

_____

_____

My prayer requests/ answers: _____

_____

_____

_____

WORDS FROM BIRDS

"Amen, Hallelujah, Praise the Lord"

When I was a little girl I wanted a parrot just like many other little kids. I mean, who doesn't? A bird that talks…. Repeats what you say… how cool is that? Not to mention they are beautiful. When you say you like parrots, you can be talking about a wide array of birds. The parrots are a broad order of more than 350 birds. Macaws, Amazons, lorikeets, lovebirds, cockatoos and many others are all considered parrots. Many parrots are kept as pets, especially macaws, Amazon parrots, cockatiels, parakeets, and cockatoos. These birds have been popular companions throughout history because they are intelligent, charismatic, colorful, and musical. Although similar, not all of these birds can reproduce human speech; those are the kind that I would have wanted. The male African gray parrot is the most accomplished user of human speech in the animal world; this rain forest-dweller is an uncanny mimic.

A mimic, copycat, imitator or your words… fun? Yes, I am sure it can be but a parrot only says what it hears and what it is taught. You can't carry on a conversation with this bird because it can only say what it has heard. The parrot says what it hears; it doesn't attach any meaning to the words that come out of its mouth. An un-responsible owner could even teach the unsuspecting creature to repeat profanities and it would do so, without being aware of any weight that its words contain. Words, phrases and even names are stated and sound so cute.

Rehearsed phrases are cute for a parrot but not for a Christian. Many people have grown up in church their entire life and have learned everything parrot style. They know just what to say to be "church" correct. "Amen, Hallelujah, Praise the Lord, and even I am praying for you" are very common churchy phrases. These phrases are not bad but if said "parrot style", without true meaning, they can be hurtful. We need to not only talk the talk, we need to walk the walk. Do these parrot Christians sound the same at work as they do at church? Do they mean what they say? Remember that God knows our heart and we need to be genuine with these phrases. Don't be a parrot Christian…. Think about what you say and mean it! Those around you will appreciate it.

Seed from the Feeder: Matthew 23:28 "In the same way on the outside you appear to people as righteous but on the inside you are full of hypocrisy and wickedness."

Flap or Fly? Think about your speech when you are with a group of believers. Do you fall into a pattern of rehearsed phrases? Have you ever told someone, "I will pray for you" then walked away and forgot? We need to be cautious and use genuine words and phrases around all people.

FEATHERED FACT: A parrot's average lifespan, in the wild, is up to an astounding 80 years!!! Domesticated birds can live 100 years or more!

Photo Credit- Zachary Shaffer

∞ **Reflection Page** ∞

Journal your thoughts: _____

_____
_____
_____
_____
_____

God, help me to: _____

_____
_____
_____

Thank you Lord for: _____

_____
_____
_____

My prayer requests/ answers: _____

_____
_____
_____

"Worn"

I know most of us can relate to this word at some point of our journey on this earth. There are many reasons we can feel overwhelmingly fatigued. It may be right now as you read this, others may reflect back a few years and some may face it in the future. It may be due to young children, broken relationships, aging parents and countless other reasons. Regardless of timing, life deals some hard blows that can keep even an eagle grounded.

Eagles like most birds go through a regular, annual molting process which consists of shedding old feathers and awaiting development of new. The eagle is aware of when this is needed and will pluck the worn feathers, go to a body of water and cleanse themselves of dirt and lice then rest in a high place and await new growth. Some feathers can take 40 days to be replaced. Plucking the feathers probably involves some pain and waiting for new feathers takes patience. Do you know where I am going here?

When you and I are worn, tired and unable to "fly", our process should be similar. First, we need to pluck out what is holding us back. Habits, people, addictions, or any number of things could be hindering our flight. Then we need to cleanse our self by going to our high place, our Father. We may need to wait for new growth and we will probably have some pain but the process will be worth the discomfort and time. If we are ever going to soar again we can't be worn, we need to be renewed!

Seed from the Feeder: Psalm 51:10 "Create in me a pure heart O God, and renew a steadfast spirit within me."

Flap or Fly?: Un-forgiveness, bitterness, sinful behavior are all areas that wear us down and make us ineffective. Take some time to talk with God today about where you are worn, what needs to be plucked from your life and allow new growth to start today!

FEATHERED FACT: The large flight feathers in the wings are replaced slowly over time, and often in pairs, one from the same position on each wing so that flight is not affected.

Photo Credit- Chuck Mason

WORDS FROM BIRDS

"Shut your Beak"

There are 23 species of vultures, 16 Old World types found in Africa, Asia and Europe, and 7 New World species found in the United States all of which share some very unusual and disgusting traits. These birds, regardless of species eat only from wounded animals or carcasses, never live animals. They search for food in groups called venues and if the group is circling it is called a kettle. By finding food in a group and only selecting weakened or dead animals they have to work less. Once they attack, they use their beaks and talons to tear at the meal. The vulture is not as strong as the eagle because they only attack an animal that is close to or already dead. Since the vulture never attacks live prey, their beaks and talons do not get used as strenuously as other hunting birds and they are weaker. So.... the weak bird must stalk and feed on weak prey, ripping at the poor defenseless creatures.

Human nature is similar to the vulture's habits. Why is it people choose to prey on other who are weakened or in bad situations? Let's consider a woman whose husband left her for another woman and now she is facing divorce and being a single mother to four children. The correct action for us is to encourage her, pray for her and help in any way that we can. But, many people, especially women in groups, choose to chat about her misfortunes and tear her down. Before you know it, she is the object of rumors and people are whispering behind her back at church. This woman is weak and wounded and the people around her are ripping her apart with their "beaks". Our mouths are our beaks and we need to offer life with it, not death and if we can't we should keep it shut!

Seed from the Feeder: Ephesians 4:29 "Do not let any unwholesome talk come out of your mouths, but only what is helpful for building others up according to their needs, that it may benefit those who listen."

Flap or Fly? As a kid, the phrase "sticks and stones may break my bones but words will never hurt me" never made sense and now as an adult, it still doesn't. Words are powerful and can be so hurtful. Are you a vulture and rip others apart with your mouth? Commit today to be positive with your mouth or keep your beak shut.

FEATHERED FACT- The vulture can eat up to 20% of its body weight in one sitting.

Photo Credit- pixabay.com

"Captivity or Freedom?"

Our extended family lives near the Toledo Zoo in Toledo, Ohio and we visit the zoo often around the holidays to see their impressive light display and a few of the animals still on exhibition. One of the displays that is still available in the winter months is an enclosure with two adult bald eagles in it. I can't help but look at them because I obviously love the bird, but I am sickened to see them in a cage and not free to soar as intended. Now, a sign clearly explains that they were wounded, saved, and were unable to return to the wild but I unfortunately know what captivity does to an eagle.

If an eagle is held in captivity it is not the same bird. Losing freedom will change the bird's personality. A captive eagle will not clean themselves, they lose their aggression and they become lazy. Captivity will obviously weaken the bird because it is unable to use the muscles that it typically uses to fly, hunt, clean game and survive. When muscles are not used, they shrink and become weak. The eagle is anything but weak when in nature, but in a cage, the eagle is entirely different and they certainly can't soar.

I believe wholeheartedly that all people are God's children and are called to be like the eagle. We are also not intended to be held in captivity or in bondage but so many of us are. The amount of addictions, divorce, suicide, depression and abuse within the church is mind boggling. Satan does not want God to win, although even he knows the end of the story. But that doesn't mean he is going to stop trying to mess us up and quit tempting us to go where we know we shouldn't? No! Satan is truly like a lion and he prowls around and preys on our weaknesses. God is stronger, but Satan will feed you lies and get you to believe otherwise. Which do you choose….

Freedom or captivity?

Seed from the Feeder: John 8:36 "For if the Son sets you free, you will be free indeed."

Flap or Fly? So, are you free or in captivity? Maybe Satan has always had a hold on you and you have never made a decision for Christ, now is the time! Or perhaps you have had a call on your life and Satan has taken you down a path of bondage. Today is your day! Choose freedom and fly free!

FEATHERED FACT: The average lifespan of an eagle in the wild is around 20 years, while in captivity they have been known to live 28 years. One eagle in captivity in the state of New York lived 50 years.

WORDS FROM BIRDS

Photo Credit- Rachel Pearch

∞ **Reflection Page** ∞

Journal your thoughts: _____

_____

_____

_____

_____

_____

God, help me to: _____

_____

_____

_____

Thank you Lord for: _____

_____

_____

_____

My prayer requests/ answers: _____

_____

_____

_____

"Let the Water Roll Off"

Our family loves going to the lake in the summer to relax, reconnect and enjoy the views. One of my favorite views is when the duck families come for a visit. Some may view them as a nuisance as they can mess up the beach but I personally enjoy watching both the adults and the duckling swim, bob in the waves and dive under for small fish and bugs. No matter how many times those ducks go under, every time they hit the surface the water just rolls off those feathers. It is amazing and one of the reasons that ducks spend the majority of their day in the water. Their feathers are barriers to the water and the damaging effects it could have on their body. If you or I spent even a portion of the day in the lake without a break, our skin would be wrinkled, pruned and not very healthy looking.

Words can be as damaging to our emotions as water is to our skin. It can be a lack of encouragement, a direct insult or a rumor, but all are destructive to our self-esteem and self- worth. It is certainly not an easy task to not allow words to pierce us and affect our feelings. We are human and naturally crave approval and acceptance from others that surround us.

Jesus was human too and unfortunately experienced the sting and cruelty of harsh words. I am sure we can't imagine what He faced in the few days and hours preceding his crucifixion. How did He endure it? Christ knew that the Father was in control and had a plan. With that knowledge, He was able to keep his eyes focused on God and the ultimate plan, allowing the meaningless words of others to roll off.

So how do we mimic the duck? The answer is to be like Christ and keep our eyes on the Father. He needs to be our sole concern and unit of measurement for our worth. Christ created us, loves us and protects us. When we grasp how great his love is for us, we have the strength to endure and eventually the comments from others seem less and less significant. So, focus on your maker and grow some duck feathers…. let the water roll off!

Seed from the Feeder: 2 Corinthians 4:18 "So we fix our eyes not on what is seen, but on what is unseen. For what is seen is temporary, but what is unseen is temporary."

WORDS FROM BIRDS

Flap or Fly? How affected are you by the words of other people? Think carefully about your interactions with others and consider the last time you were hurt by someone's comments towards you. Now, ponder how your reaction may have been different if you care only about Jesus' assessment of you. Next time you are faced with tough words, turn to the face of Christ and let the word of man roll off your back.

FEATHERED FACT- The mallard is thought to be the most abundant and wide-ranging duck on Earth.

Photo Credit- Tawnya Shaffer

∞ Reflection Page ∞

Journal your thoughts: _____

_____

_____

_____

_____

_____

God, help me to: _____

_____

_____

_____

Thank you Lord for: _____

_____

_____

_____

My prayer requests/ answers: _____

_____

_____

_____

WORDS FROM BIRDS

"Fiercely Committed"

The eagle is a hunter, a family bird, a survivor, and is strongly committed to all of these endeavors. The eagle rarely migrates and often has to endure the harshness and cruelty that winter brings. Game can become scarce and when they do seize a meal, they will protect it fiercely. If someone or something threatens an eagle's young, they will strongly defend them. The feet of the eagle are key to this fierceness. The feet of the eagle are key to its aggressiveness in the hunt and in defensive strategies. Each foot has 4 toes, 3 facing forward and 1 facing back that works like our thumbs. The feet are covered by a scaly, yellow covering called pod theca that protects the feet from injury when struggling with prey. At the end of each toe is an extremely sharp and strong talon. Even with the everyday wear and tear, an eagle's talons can be 2 inches long. Many people think that the beak is what kills the prey but it is really the talons. The eagle will drive the talons deep into the carcass to pierce vital organs. The grip of the talon is extremely strong and can kill prey just from the force of the grasp. To assist the hold on slippery fish, there is a spiny tipped pad in the soles of the toes called papillae. All of these features make the grip of an eagle extremely strong.

How is your grip? Are you strongly committed to your family? Is your faith a top priority and no matter what comes your way you won't let go? I know we don't possess talons but we do have free will. With that free will comes the choice to be committed no matter what. Moses wandered for 40 years with complainers and grumblers and never let go of his commitment to God. Esther risked her life to save her people. Holding on to what is right is hard and tiring but the rewards are eternal!

Seed from the Feeder: Proverbs 16:3 "Commit to the Lord whatever you do, and your plans will succeed."

Flap or Fly? Commitment is not easy! It involves sacrifice, endurance and tenacity. Alone we don't have the strength to stay committed in this world but with the help of God we can! Be fiercely committed to your family and your God! Don't let go no matter what!

FEATHERED FACT: Like the bill, talons grow continuously but everyday activities such as hunting and perching, wear down talons and keep them from getting too long.

WORDS FROM BIRDS

Photo Credit- Karl Wehner

∞ **Reflection Page** ∞

Journal your thoughts: _____

_____

_____

_____

_____

_____

God, help me to: _____

_____

_____

_____

Thank you Lord for: _____

_____

_____

_____

My prayer requests/ answers: _____

_____

_____

_____

"Wave Runner Attack"

One summer several years ago, I was riding our wave runner with my daughter behind me. We were having a great time jumping waves and swerving back and forth. We went for a spin in the cove near the home of a pair of swans. Apparently we got a little too close for their liking because instead of screams of exhilaration, my daughter was shrieking with fear. "Faster, faster mom!" she yelled. I glanced back and found the large male swan flying low and rapidly approaching my daughters head. So, I hit the throttle hard and eventually the big, beautiful bird conceded and headed back to his mate and nest. Needless to say, my daughter has not been a fan of the swan since that day.

The swan is a beautiful, regal bird but can be territorial and downright mean when threatened. Unfortunately, people can be "beautiful" on the outside and malicious simultaneously. So many "swan Christians" can appear to be kind, loving, and know just what to say and then turn around and be unkind and just plain mean to others. How is that possible? Do they think that as long as the pastor, their parents or the members of their small group aren't watching, it doesn't count if they don't treat that waitress with love? Will it matter if they are short tempered with the cashier as long as people they know don't find out? The answer is a resounding "YES" it does matter. Jesus knows your heart and you may fool those around you but you will never fool Him.

Keeping up a perfect appearance doesn't matter if your heart is callous and unkind. Have people approached you because they thought you were attractive like the swan only to be met with unpleasant and despicable behavior? Work to make your inside as beautiful as the outside.

Seed from the Feeder: 1 Samuel 16:7b "The Lord does not look at the things man looks at. Man looks at the outward appearance but the Lord looks at the heart."

Flap or Fly? It is time for a little honest self-reflection. How does your inside beauty compare to your outside appearance? Do people see the real you in your everyday behavior? Is how you act on Sunday the same as how you act on Monday? Christ knows your heart…. does it need some attention today?

FEATHERED FACT- Most swan pair bonds are formed when swans are 4 to 7 years old, although some pairs do not form until they are nearly 20 years old. "Divorces" have been known between birds, in which case the mates will breed with different birds in differing breeding seasons. Occasionally, if his mate dies, a male Trumpeter Swan may not pair again for the rest of his life.

WORDS FROM BIRDS

Photo Credit- Tawnya Shaffer

∞ **Reflection Page** ∞

Journal your thoughts: _____

_____

_____

_____

_____

_____

_____

God, help me to: _____

_____

_____

_____

_____

Thank you Lord for: _____

_____

_____

_____

_____

My prayer requests/ answers: _____

_____

_____

_____

_____

"Flight School"

Eaglets are 3-4 ounces when they are hatched and by 6 weeks they are a foot tall. By 12 weeks they are practice flying and are expected to be flying on their own soon after that. Like children, some eagles need more encouragement than others. If the young eagles are not taking to flight on their own the parents will "push them out of the nest" in their own way. One of the parents will take the young eagle on their back, fly to a certain height, and then drop them. Yes, I did say they drop them. The goal of course is to get them to spread their wings and start flying. What happens if the eaglet doesn't fly? Is it crash and burn? No, just in time one of the parents will sweep in and catch the young bird. So, is it back to the nest? Oh no…. back up they go and the process is repeated until that young eagle learns to soar. Why are the parents so determined to get that youngster to fly? The parents know that survival is tough and their offspring will have to get it right and soon. In some regions, up to 50% of young eagles die in this initial period away from the nest. The parents have been there and want to prevent any disaster. Basically, mom & dad are helping junior to survive on his own.

Our heavenly Father is equally concerned with our wellbeing and our survival. Many of us have been called to do something for God and we are staying in the security of the nest. How many of us want the insecurity and uncertainty of "flying on our own"? Probably not too many. But remember, even if you start to fall, your Father will be there to swoop you up and catch you. None of us will ever soar if we don't get out of the nest.

Seed from the Feeder: Deuteronomy 32:11 "Like an eagle that stirs up its nest and hovers over its young, that spreads its wings to catch them and carries them on its pinions."

Flap or Fly? God has an amazing plan for you! We are truly each destined for something and when you are prompted to act don't stay in the safety of the nest. You are built for greatness and built to soar but you will never experience the wind under your wings if they are folded and in the security of the nest! Fly and trust God to catch you!

FEATHERED FACT- Learning to catch prey is harder than learning to fly. Juvenile eagles will continue to follow their parents around for some time watching them and practicing their new skills until they are stronger and have learned how to hunt.

WORDS FROM BIRDS

Photo credit: Pam Oberski

∞ Reflection Page ∞

Journal your thoughts: _____

_____

_____

_____

_____

_____

_____

God, help me to: _____

_____

_____

_____

Thank you Lord for: _____

_____

_____

_____

My prayer requests/ answers: _____

_____

_____

_____

"A Call to Remember"

The day was sunny, breezy and typically perfect for an April day in Indiana. I wished that my mood matched the weather but instead I had been crying and was facing a major trial and crossroad in my life. Regardless of the sunshine, I felt gloomy and hopeless. I sat on my deck allowing the sun to warm me when I heard a familiar call; "Oo-wah-hooo – hoo- hoo" came the consistent call. I looked up to see a graceful mourning dove looking down on me from the roof of our garage. The sound took me back to my childhood when I would hear the same sound and search for the dove which I knew was nearby. The mourning dove obtained its name because of the sad, slow, sound of its unchanging coo that some say sounds like it is crying. In reality this call is from the male dove that is searching for a lifelong mate. For me, the sweet sound matched my mood and I found comfort in my gray feathered friend.

For the next several days, I would be outside working in the yard and I would hear my friend's call. He would be perched on a roof or high branch but I could always find him. As my difficult time pressed on, I began to see a parallel and a comfort in this sweet songbird. In Mark 1:10 scripture tells us that "As Jesus was coming up out of the water, he saw the heaven being torn open and the Spirit descending on Him like a dove." We are promised as Christians that we receive the Holy Spirit when we accept Christ as our savior. He exists to be a comforter and help to us here on earth. Repeatedly in scripture, like in Mark, the Holy Spirit is referenced as a dove.

A moment of realization and truth hit me the next time I saw my cooing friend. Despite my situation, regardless of how dark it may seem, the Holy Spirit is with me. Just like my dove friend who I visibly enjoyed, my Comforter is with me at all times and will carry me through any trial I experience. I still see my dove friend and each time I hear that "Oo-wah-hooo – hoo- hoo" I thank God for the reminder that I am not alone.

Seed from the Feeder: John 14:26-27 "But the Counselor, the Holy Spirit, whom the Father will send in my name, will teach you all things and will remind you of everything I have said to you. Peace I leave with you; my peace I give you. I do not give to you as the world gives. Do not let your hearts be troubled and do not be afraid."

Flap or Fly? Are you going through a tough time? Is your life full of chaos or peace? I encourage you to stop and listen for the comfort of the Holy Spirit. He is present and a comforter in times of trouble. Listen for His call!

FEATHERED FACT- Their long, pointed wings are almost falcon-like in appearance, while their pointed tails are longer than those of any other doves. These "design features" enable the birds to fly fast. Mourning doves have been clocked at 55 mph!

Photo Credit- Tawnya Shaffer

∞ **Reflection Page** ∞

Journal your thoughts: _____

_____

_____

_____

_____

_____

God, help me to: _____

_____

_____

_____

Thank you Lord for: _____

_____

_____

_____

My prayer requests/ answers: _____

_____

_____

_____

"Built in GPS"

My only daughter recently got her driver's license and has been doing very well finding her way around, staying safe and keeping her mother from fretting too much. She is the youngest and I had been through the new driver phase twice before but she is my baby and the only girl so I guess it is natural to worry some. All was well until her first trip to voice lessons which is located 35 minutes north on the expressway and through traffic. I gave her written directions but did not have a GPS to send with her. We talked it through and she seemed confident. I told her to call if she needed anything. Almost 30 minutes passed and then I got the call, "Mom, I am not sure where I am," she confessed. I reassured her and after quizzing her, we discovered that instead of going north on the interstate, she had gone south, the complete distance that she should have travelled north. With her voice lesson now more than an hour away from her location, I instructed her to turn around and just come home. She felt horrible but I explained that directions are difficult to grasp at times and that she would get it eventually.

The eagle knows direction well. It is born into them. They are born with a liquid in their eye that actually hardens as they mature. This solution acts as a compass and when the eagle goes the wrong way, it causes a low level of pain to keep them on track. What a great tool. Couldn't most of that use that in our spiritual life? It would be great to have a spiritual compass that is built into us at birth and anytime that we wander away, we would feel a low level of pain and return to what we know to be true.

In some ways, I feel we have that in the Holy Spirit. He is our guide and sometimes when we venture off the path the result is pain. The question is do we listen to the warning? My daughter didn't have a GPS with her to turn her around. We have a built in GPS through the Holy Spirit but no GPS is effective unless the user listens to the directions it gives! Are you listening to your spiritual compass?

Seed from the Feeder: Proverbs 22:6 "Train a child in the way he should go, and when he is old he will not depart from it."

Flap or Fly? Are you listening to God's direction in your life? How much time do you spend asking Him for things versus how much time do you spend listening? We will never hear God's voice if we never stop talking. Tune in to your spiritual GPS today.

WORDS FROM BIRDS

FEATHERED FACT- The primary and flight feathers of juvenile eagles are several inches longer than those of the adults making them seem bigger than their parents. The longer feathers provide more surface area which assists the young eagles while they master the art of flying.

Photo credit- Pam Oberski

∞ **Reflection Page** ∞

Journal your thoughts: _____

_____

_____

_____

_____

_____

_____

God, help me to: _____

_____

_____

_____

Thank you Lord for: _____

_____

_____

_____

My prayer requests/ answers: _____

_____

_____

_____

"Victim of a Dive Attack"

As a teenager, one of my chores was to mow our very large yard with our riding mower. I loved being outside and actually enjoyed the time I spent on that big, yellow tractor. We had over ten acres and at least four of them had to be manicured. So out I went regularly to commune with nature and the hum of the mower. The majority of the time it was very peaceful until I came across my friends the killdeers. Typically it was not a friendly encounter. I would be mowing along and all of a sudden a brown and white blur would come diving at my head. So much for peaceful! These long legged- little birds are considered shorebirds, but they often live far from water. They choose grassy habitats such as fields, meadows, and my yard to nest in. The nest itself is merely a shallow depression or bowl in the ground, fringed by some stones and blades of grass. Not the safest home for the young ones. The nest is well camouflaged, as the spots of the eggs disguise them as stones, so my attacks were often unannounced because I rarely saw the nest until I was too close.

Because the killdeer is very sensitive to activity near their nests they will challenge the object creating the threat, in this case me. Sometimes these little actors will perform a "broken wing act" that looks like they are injured and is intended to distract predators from the nest. More than once, these little characters fooled me into thinking that I may have ran over them with my blades. I would start to feel horrible and then the feathered performer would fly off, perfectly fine. You would think that they would just learn to be like other birds and put their nests in or at least under a tree….. but no, every year was the same. With spring came the dive attacks.

In the Bible, it talks about building a strong foundation for your faith. The killdeer did not choose a wise foundation and I am sure countless eggs are destroyed every year. What is your faith built on? A strong foundation with Jesus Christ or something of the world?

Seed from the Feeder: Matthew 7:24 "Therefore everyone who hears these words of mine and puts them into practice is like a wise man who built His house on the rock."

Flap or Fly? Are you the wise man or the foolish man in the Bible? It says that the wise man listens to and practices the law of God but the foolish man ignores them. Which are you? Is your nest on the ground and being mowed over or is your nest high and protected?

WORDS FROM BIRDS

FEATHERED FACT- Killdeer are easily alarmed; their piercing warning cries often panic other nearby birds.

Photo Credit- pixabay.com

∞ **Reflection Page** ∞

Journal your thoughts: _____

_____

_____

_____

_____

_____

God, help me to: _____

_____

_____

_____

Thank you Lord for: _____

_____

_____

_____

My prayer requests/ answers: _____

_____

_____

_____

"Fresh Meat Please"

My middle child was a very picky eater when he was younger. He would not eat vegetables, only bananas for fruit, no pasta, but he ate a lot of meat as long as it was plain. His favorite was chicken nuggets, which in some situations cannot be considered true meat but he ate them. So we began to cut up turkey, ham, and beef in small pieces and they became turkey nuggets, ham nuggets and beef nuggets. It actually worked for a while. He continued his very select diet until he was a teenager and he began trying and liking more food.

The eagle enjoys a select diet but for very good reasons. His diet consists of a lot of fish if the eagle's home is near a body of water. Along with fish, small animals such as mice, rabbits, fox, squirrels and ducks make an acceptable meal. Unlike the vulture, the eagle strongly prefers to eat fresh prey. He will rarely eat a rotting carcass that has been lying around. Eagles have been known to eat road kill if it is fairly fresh and if there are no better options such as in winter when pickings are slim. If the eagle does eat something bad, it will fly to a high place like a rock, and spread itself out in a ritual called "sunning" and wait until the toxins are reabsorbed out of its body.

What do Christians do when we make wrong choices? Do we keep trying to fly or do we take time to rid ourselves of the bad? How selective is your diet? Are you putting things into your body that are God honoring or are you filling yourself with damaging and sinful items that seek to destroy? Remember that our body is the temple of the Holy Spirit. Christ lives within us. If you were having Christ over for dinner I am sure the menu would be impeccable yet daily we fill our body, His home, with deplorable choices. Start choosing a healthy spiritual diet.

Seed from the Feeder: Romans 12:1 "Therefore I urge you brothers, in view of God's mercy, to offer your bodies as living sacrifices, holy and pleasing to God, which is our spiritual worship.

Flap or Fly? Are you filling yourself with devotions, scripture and Christian music or are you listening to worldly music, watching questionable TV and using the computer for activities that are less than pleasing to God? All of those are your spiritual diet. Is it time to make some changes?

FEATHERED FACT- Eagles can only lift and carry about half of their body weight.

WORDS FROM BIRDS

Photo Credit- Adam Anastasoff

∞ **Reflection Page** ∞

Journal your thoughts: _____

_____
_____
_____
_____
_____

God, help me to: _____

_____
_____
_____

Thank you Lord for: _____

_____
_____
_____

My prayer requests/ answers: _____

_____
_____
_____

"The Un-Bird"

If you haven't caught on yet, I am a bit of a bird enthusiast and rarely fail to notice any feathered friend nearby. In all my time studying and researching birds, there is one fowl that has perplexed me. Now before I go any further, please know that it is not that I dislike this little bird, I am just amazed by its differences to most other birds. It is probably one of the most recognized birds in the world and is often showcased in zoos, but you will not find it in the aviary, you will find it in its own enclosure by water not open air. The bird I am referring to is the penguin.

The penguin is a cute and curious little fellow but is vastly different from other birds, especially the eagle. First, it is completely flightless and does most of its moving about in the water where it finds 100% of its food source. Secondly, the penguins eyes work better in the water than in the air leaving it a bit vulnerable to predators while on land since it cannot see as well and cannot move quickly. Thirdly, where most birds spend time in the air or in trees, the penguin spends 75% of life at sea. Lastly, the parent penguin does not build nests for its young, but rather incubates the eggs at their feet in a flap called a brood pouch. Incubation takes 8-10 weeks to complete. So, the differences between a penguin and the majority of birds are many.

This little "un-bird" as I have titled it, has feathers, a beak and lays eggs but acts completely different than most of its feathered friends. Like I said, it is adorable but it just does not seem to be a bird to me.

So, what makes the penguin a bird? The traits that I mentioned above make it a bird. But its actions make the penguin seem more aquatic than bird-like. People may have a Bible, a cross necklace and even a church membership but their behavior may not be Christian like at all. What makes a person a Christian? A true heart decision to follow Jesus Christ. You may put that cross necklace on but nothing else you do or say reflects Jesus? Are you a true Christian or an "Un-Christian?" Only God can judge the condition of your heart and if you are a bird ready to soar for Him!

Seed from the Feeder: 2 Corinthians 5:10 "We must all appear before the judgment seat of Christ, that each one may receive what is due him for the things done while in the body, whether good or bad."

Flap or Fly? Many people state that they are Christians and love God but don't act at all like a Christian. It is not for man to judge if you are saved or not. That is between you and God. Take time today to talk to God. If you haven't asked Him into your life, don't wait another minute. If you have, be sure you are acting like the bird He has called you to be.

FEATHERED FACT- Penguins have a thick layer of insulating feathers that keeps them warm in water and they also are able to control blood flow to their extremities, reducing the amount of blood that gets cold, but still keeping the extremities from freezing.

Photo Credit- Tawnya Shaffer

∞ **Reflection Page** ∞

Journal your thoughts: _____

_____

_____

_____

_____

_____

God, help me to: _____

_____

_____

_____

Thank you Lord for: _____

_____

_____

_____

My prayer requests/ answers: _____

_____

_____

_____

"Flying Solo"

My oldest son went on several international mission trips alone, while he was still in high school. Of course, mom was a bit anxious, especially the one summer when he had a month of boot camp and a month to be spent in New Zealand and Australia. Sure, those places are great and I would love to visit them too but he was only 17 and was traveling with people he didn't know. It didn't sway him. He was convinced that is where God wanted him so off he went to travel the world. I was proud of his courage and ability to venture out and it reminded me of the majestic and bold eagle.

The eagle is not a bird that has to travel in flocks. He is perfectly content by himself and eventually with a mate after 5-7 years. Sometimes the eagle will live in a small community if there are juvenile eagles still in the area but they are not a flock type of bird. The penguin, flamingo, and many other birds find comfort in numbers because they are unable to defend themselves against predators. The eagle is equipped to handle adversity and attackers that come against it. He is bold, strong and fiercely committed and has the ability to soar.

The eagle is actually territorial especially during nesting season and will defend its territory boldly. Depending on the food and the number of eagles in the area, a typical territory is 1-2 square miles, larger when there is less food available. A flock is not welcome by the eagle, he needs to fly alone.

Are you an eagle? Are you able or maybe I should say willing to be set apart from others? A lot of people prefer the comfort of a group. It is easier to go with the flow and just fit in with those around you. Christians are a minority in this big world and we are often called to stand alone, defend our faith and act courageously. It isn't always easy but the rewards are so worth it. My son was willing to fly solo at a young age. How about you?

Seed from the Feeder: Matthew 5:16 "Let your light shine before men that they may see your good deeds and praise your father in heaven."

Flap or Fly? It is time to fly for Jesus! Stop being a chicken, vulture, blue jay or whatever bird you related to. Don't listen to the ones who keep dragging you back into bad habits. Step out, be bold for Jesus and fly solo if you are called to. Remember even if the eagle is the only bird around, God is helping him to soar! Fly solo and fly strong for Christ!

FEATHERED FACT- **Sometimes a stronger or more dominant eagle will challenge another for the same territory. Fights can last from 2 hours to 2 days and the victor takes the residency of the territory as well as the opportunity to breed. The observing mate does not interfere with the fighting.**

Photo Credit- Karl Wehner

∞ **Reflection Page** ∞

Journal your thoughts: _____

_____

_____

_____

_____

_____

God, help me to: _____

_____

_____

_____

Thank you Lord for: _____

_____

_____

_____

My prayer requests/ answers: _____

_____

_____

_____

WORDS FROM BIRDS

Bibliography

- http://ecolocalizer.com
- http://animals.nationalgeographic.com
- http://en.wikipedia.org
- http://birdsandbloomsblog.com
- http://birding.about.com
- http://www.baldeagleinfo.com
- "Majestic Eagles, Compelling facts and Images of the Bald Eagle" by Stan Tekiela; copyright 2007, Adventure Publications Inc.
- http://pixaby.com

Contact Information:

For more information or to contact Tawnya for speaking engagements, please use either thesoarspot.com or find me on Facebook at Tawnya Shaffer Ministries. Blessings!

WORDS FROM BIRDS

Made in the USA
Lexington, KY
17 December 2017